The Ultimate
Pecan Recipe Book

Discover New Different and Delicious
Ways to Use Pecans!

BY: Allie Allen

COOK & ENJOY

Copyright 2019 Allie Allen

Copyright Notes

This book is written as an informational tool. While the author has taken every precaution to ensure the accuracy of the information provided therein, the reader is warned that they assume all risk when following the content. The author will not be held responsible for any damages that may occur as a result of the readers' actions.

The author does not give permission to reproduce this book in any form, including but not limited to: print, social media posts, electronic copies or photocopies, unless permission is expressly given in writing.

Table of Contents

Introduction

Whether you're looking for a recipe for your next party or want to use up all those pecans you have in stock, look no further than this recipe book. You'll find 30 of the most mouth-watering pecan recipes, complete with simple ingredients and detailed instructions.

Thanks to this book, you will be able to put up everything from classic pecan pie to sinfully addicting hummingbird cupcakes. So, what are you waiting for? Select a recipe and let's begin!

1. Pecan Oreo Granola

Keep plenty of this crispy granola on hand to top ice cream or oatmeal, or to simply munch on as a satisfying snack.

Makes: 5 cups

Prep: 10 mins

Cook: 25 mins

Ingredients:

- 2 cups rolled oats
- ½ cup flaked coconut
- ½ cup pecans, chopped
- 3 tbsp. honey
- 4 tsp. orange juice
- 16 Oreos, chopped

Directions:

Preheat the oven to 300°F.

Combine together the oats, coconut, pecan, honey and orange juice in a large baking pan.

Bake for 15 minutes. Remove and stir and then bake for 10 minutes more. Cool.

Add in the chopped Oreos and mix until well combined.

2. Pecan Pie Oatmeal

The flavors of your favorite pie come together to form the most insanely delicious oatmeal recipe ever.

Makes: 2 servings

Prep: 2 mins

Cook: 5 mins

Ingredients:

- 1 cup quick-cooking oats
- 2 1/2 cups milk
- 1 tsp vanilla extract
- 1/3 cup chopped pecans, plus extra for topping
- 1 ½ tsp maple syrup
- ½ tsp brown sugar
- ½ tsp ground cinnamon
- Pinch of nutmeg

Directions:

In a medium-sized saucepan, combine oats, milk, vanilla extract, pecans, maple syrup, brown sugar, cinnamon and nutmeg over medium-high heat. Bring mixture to a boil, lower and cook for 5 minutes.

Remove pan from heat. Divide between bowls and top with additional pecans.

3. Coffee Ice Cream with Caramelized Pecans

Coffee and sweetened nuts make a mouth-watering combination.

Makes: 4-6 servings

Prep: 2 hrs. 10 mins

Cook: 20 mins

Ingredients:

For the ice cream:

- 1 ¼ cups milk
- 1 tbsp. demerara sugar
- 6 tbsp. finely ground coffee or 1 tbsp. instant coffee granules
- 1 egg plus 2 yolks
- 1 ¼ cups heavy cream
- 1 tbsp. caster sugar

For the pecans:

- 1 cup pecan halves
- 4 tbsp. soft dark brown sugar

Directions:

Heat the 1 1/4 cups milk and sugar in a small pan to boiling point. Remove and add in the coffee. Leave for 2 mins, then stir, cover and allow to cool.

Beat the egg and yolks until the mixture is thick and pale.

Strain the coffee mixture into a clean pan, heat to boiling point, then pour on to the eggs in a stream, beating hard.

Set over pot of simmering water and whisk until thickened. Cool, then chill in the fridge.

Whip the cream with the caster sugar, Fold it into the coffee custard and freeze in a covered container. Beat twice at hourly intervals, then leave to freeze firm.

To caramelize the nuts, preheat the oven to 350°F. Spread pecans on a baking pan and place in the oven for 10 minutes.

On the top of the stove, dissolve the brown sugar in 2 tbsp. water in a heavy-based pan, shaking it about over a low heat until the sugar dissolves completely and the syrup clears.

When the syrup begins to bubble, tip in the toasted pecans and cook for a minute or two over a medium heat until the syrup coats and clings to the nuts.

Spread the nuts on a lightly oiled baking sheet, separating them with the tip of a knife, and leave to cool.

Remove ice cream from the freezer 15 minutes before scooping it into portions and serving with caramelized pecans.

4. Pumpkin Spice Pecan Fudge

A perfect fudge recipe for the holiday season, this recipe is easy and absolutely divine.

Makes: 25 servings

Prep: 5 mins plus chilling time

Cook: 5 mins

Ingredients:

- 18 oz. pumpkin spice morsels
- 1 14 oz. can of sweetened condensed milk
- Dash of salt
- 1 tsp. vanilla extract
- 1 cup pecans, roasted, chopped and divided

Directions:

Prep an 8X8 inch pan with foil and grease lightly with cooking spray.

In a saucepan set over medium heat, add in the pumpkin spice morsels, condensed milk and dash of salt. Cook for 2 minutes or until melted. Remove and add in the vanilla and most of the pecans except for 3 tablespoons. Stir well to mix.

Pour mixture into the dish and then top with remaining pecans. Cover and refrigerate for at least 2 hours.

Slice and serve.

5. Cookie Butter Pecan Fudge

A delicious 3-ingredient fudge recipe with crunchy pecans and luscious Lotus Biscoff cookie butter.

Makes: 12 servings

Prep: 5 mins plus chilling time

Cook: 1 min

Ingredients:

- 1 14 ounce tub vanilla frosting
- 1 ½ cups Biscoff cookie butter
- ½ cup pecans, cut into halves

Directions:

Prep an 8X8 inch pan with foil and grease lightly with cooking spray.

In a large bowl, combine the cookie butter and vanilla frosting. Microwave for 1 min and then mix until smooth. Add in the pecan halves and stir again until incorporated.

Pour mixture into the baking dish.

Cover and refrigerate for 2 hrs. Slice and serve.

6. Butter Pecan Frozen Yogurt

A delicious fro-yo recipe with golden pecans.

Makes: 4 servings

Prep: 10 mins

Freezing Time: 3 hrs.

Cook: -

Ingredients:

- 2/3 cup pecans, chopped
- 3 tbsp. unsalted butter
- 4 cups yogurt
- 1 cup sugar or 1/3 cup honey
- 1 tbsp pure vanilla extract

Directions:

In a saucepan, sauté the pecans with the butter until golden, 2-3 minutes. Set aside to cool.

Combine remaining ingredients in a blender or with a mixer to make a light, smooth mixture.

Pour into a tray or ice-cube tray without the dividers.

Place in the freezer of the refrigerator at the coldest setting or a deep freezer for 30 mins-1 hr., or until the mixture is mushy but not solid.

Scrape the mixture into a cold bowl & beat it with a rotary beater or electric mixer as rapidly as possible until smooth.

Return to the tray and the freezer. When almost frozen solid, repeat the beating process. Add in the pecans.

Return to the tray and cover the cream with plastic wrap. Put in the freezer until solid.

Serve.

7. Hummingbird Cupcakes with Cream Cheese Frosting

Soft, fluffy, fruity and nutty, these cupcakes are a Southern classic joy guaranteed to please everyone!

Makes: 12 cupcakes

Prep: 15 mins

Bake: 20 mins

Ingredients:

For the cupcakes:

- 1 1/2 cups all-purpose flour
- 3/4 cup white sugar
- 1/2 tsp baking soda
- 1/2 tsp ground cinnamon
- 1/4 tsp salt
- 1/4 tsp ground cardamom
- 1 large egg
- 1/4 cup unsweetened applesauce
- 1 1/2 vegetable oil
- 2 large or 3 small-medium bananas, peeled and mashed
- 4 ounces crushed pineapple, undrained
- 1 tsp vanilla extract
- 1/2 cup chopped pecans

For the frosting:

- ½ cup unsalted butter, softened
- 1 ¾ cups icing sugar
- ⅛ tsp salt
- ½ tsp vanilla extract
- 1 cup cream cheese, cold and cut into cubes
- Chopped pecans, for decoration

Directions:

For the cupcakes:

Preheat oven to 350°F & set a cupcake pan with 12 liners.

In a medium-sized bowl, combine dry ingredients. Set aside.

In a large bowl, combine applesauce, oil, bananas, pineapple and vanilla extract. Add in the egg and whisk until smooth. Add in the dry ingredients and whisk until just combined. Fold in chopped pecans.

Pour batter and bake for 18-22 mins.

Cool cupcakes on a cooling rack.

For the frosting:

In a large bowl, beat butter for a minute or so until creamy.

Add in the icing sugar, salt and vanilla and beat for about 6 minutes or until mixture has lightened.

Add in the cream cheese cubes one at a time, mixing well after each cube so no lumps are formed.

Beat for about 3 mins.

Frost cooled cupcakes and top with chopped pecans.

8. Chocolate Bark with Pecans and Walnuts

Make your own candy with this easy-to-follow white and dark chocolate bark recipe. Throw in dried fruits if you like!

Makes: 8 servings

Prep: 10 mins plus cooling time

Cook: -

Ingredients:

- 16 oz. dark chocolate, chopped
- 12 oz. white chocolate, chopped
- ½ cup walnuts, chopped
- ¼ cup pecans, chopped

Directions:

Line 2 baking pans with parchment paper, making sure to leave an overhang on both sides.

Place 14 oz. of the dark chocolate in a large bowl. Melt in the microwave in 20 second intervals. Add in the remaining 2 oz. of chocolate and stir until smooth. Repeat with the white chocolate.

Divide the dark chocolate evenly between the two pans and spread until a rough rectangle is formed. Add in dollops of the white chocolate and swirl using a knife.

Sprinkle on the nuts and refrigerate for about 2 hours. Peel off the paper and break bark into pieces. Serve.

9. Caramel Pecan Brownie Turtles

These cute turtle-shaped caramel pecan brownies are the perfect treat for kids.

Makes: 8 servings

Prep: 10 mins

Cook: 12 mins

Ingredients:

- 1 (18.3 ounce) package brownie mix
- ½ cup pecans, chopped
- 16 pecans, halved
- 16 butterscotch chips
- Caramel ice cream topping

Directions:

Preheat the oven to 350°F.

Prepare the brownie according to the instructions on the pack.

Stir the chopped pecans into the brownie batter.

Fill 8 mini-muffin cup and 8 regular-sized muffin cups to 2/3 capacity.

Bake in the oven for 12 minutes for mini brownies and between 22-25 minutes for the regular size, until springy to the touch. Cool completely on wire racks.

On 8 plates, place 1 regular-sized brownie (the turtle's body) and 1 mini brownie for the head.

Arrange 4 pecan halves around the turtle's body to represent its feet.

Use the butterscotch chips as eyes and drizzle with caramel topping.

Serve.

10. Pecan Pie

No pecan recipe book would be complete without the addition of a classic pecan pie recipe.

Makes: 12-16 slices

Prep: 1 ½ hrs.

Cook: 1 hr.

Ingredients:

Pie Dough:

- ¾ cup all-purpose flour, sifted
- ½ tsp. salt
- 4 ½ tbsp. cubed cold unsalted butter
- 2 tbsp. ice water

Filling:

- 4 eggs
- 1 cup light corn syrup
- 1/3 cup packed light brown sugar
- ¼ cup granulated sugar
- ¼ cup unsalted butter, melted
- 1 tsp. sea salt
- 3 cups pecan halves
- 1 tsp. vanilla extract
- For Serving:
- Vanilla ice cream or whipped cream

Directions:

Process the flour & salt in a food processor and pulse to combine.

Add the unsalted butter and pulse until the butter is broken up into lumps about the size of small peas.

Add the water, 1/2 tablespoon at a time, pulsing as you go, until the mixture has a barely sticky, dough like texture.

Move mixture to a bowl and then gently work the dough with your hands until it forms a firm ball. Shape it into a disk, cover it in plastic wrap, and chill in the refrigerator for at least 1 hour.

Preheat the oven to 375°F.

Remove the dough and let sit at on the counter for 5 minutes. On a floured surface, roll out the dough into a circle of about 13 inch. in diameter.

Gently fold the circle in 1/2, & then in half again, so it looks like a quarter wedge of a circle. Center the point of the wedge in a 10-inch pie plate and gently unfold the dough.

Trim the dough so that just 1 inch hangs over the sides. Fold the overhanging dough under itself to form a rim. Crimp this rim between your thumb and forefinger to form a patterned edge around the edges of the pie plate.

Bake the crust for 5 minutes. Remove and set it aside. This is not prebaking the crust but giving it a bit of a head start for a very wet pie filling.

Lower the oven temperature to 350 degrees. For the filling, combine the 4 eggs, corn syrup, sugars, butter, salt, and vanilla in a large bowl. Whisk until smooth. Stir in the pecans.

Pour the mixture into the pie crust.

Bake for an hour, or until the filling jiggles just slightly in the center when gently shaken.

Let the pie cool completely, approximately 2 hours, before serving. Serve with vanilla ice cream or whipped cream.

11. Cayenne Candied Pecans

Candied pecans are perfect for sprinkling on salads or mixing into ice cream. Making them is relatively easy, and they have a wonderfully long shelf life. Adding a bit of cayenne pepper to the spice blend provides a surprising kick in an otherwise sweet and crunchy treat.

Makes: 1 cup

Prep: 15 mins

Cook: 20 mins

Ingredients:

- 2 egg whites
- 1 teaspoon vanilla extract
- 1 cup whole pecans
- ¼ cup granulated sugar
- 1 tablespoon cayenne pepper
- 1 tablespoon ground cinnamon
- ½ teaspoon ground nutmeg
- ¼ cup packed brown sugar

Directions:

Preheat the oven to 350°F.

In a med bowl, whisk the egg whites until frothy. Whisk in the vanilla.

Add the pecans and stir to coat completely.

In a bowl, stir together the sugar, cayenne pepper, cinnamon, and nutmeg. Transfer half to a second small bowl and set aside.

Mix the brown sugar into one of the bowls of spiced sugar mixture. Coat the pecans evenly in the brown sugar-spiced sugar blend. Transfer them to the skillet.

Bake for 10 minutes, stir well, and bake for 10 minutes more.

Remove the pecans & add the reserved spiced sugar. Stir well to coat and let cool completely before serving.

12. Chocolate Pecan Cookie Sundaes

This dessert is decadence personified: luscious pecan-chocolate chunk cookies topped with great ice cream and salted caramel sauce.

Makes: 12 servings

Ingredients:

- 1 stick unsalted butter, softened, + butter to grease pans
- ½ cup firmly packed dark brown sugar
- ½ cup sugar
- 1 large egg
- 1 teaspoon vanilla extract
- 1 cup + 2 Tablespoons unbleached all-purpose flour
- ¼ teaspoon salt
- 1 cup coarsely chopped dark chocolate chunks (about 6 ounces)
- ½ cup coarsely chopped pecans
- ½ teaspoon of baking soda
- Salted Caramel Sauce, to serve
- Vanilla or chocolate ice cream, to serve

Directions:

Preheat your oven to 350°F. Grease as many 6-inch cast-iron skillets as you will use or a 10-inch skillet with butter.

In a bowl, cream the softened stick of butter and both sugars.

Add in the egg & vanilla. In another bowl, combine the salt, flour, and baking soda. Add the dry ingredients to the butter mix and stir until smooth. Mix in the chocolate and the pecans.

For each cookie, scoop out a level ¼-cup measure of the dough (or weigh out 2-ounce portions on a kitchen scale) and put the dough in the center of the 6-inch pan. Repeat until all the pans are filled, then put them in the oven and bake until the cookies are lightly browned, about 13 to 15 minutes. Remove the pans and let them cool until the cookies are warm, not hot.

(Alternatively, put the dough into the 10-inch skillet, flatten into a 1-inch thick disc, and bake at 325°F until done.)

Serve with ice cream and caramel sauce.

13. Cinnamon Streusel Coffee Cake

Cinnamon streusel coffee cake with a pecan and brown sugar filling.

Makes: 6-8 servings

Prep: 20 mins

Cook: 45 mins

Ingredients:

Filling:

- 1½ cups packed brown sugar
- 1 cup chopped pecans
- ½ cup all-purpose flour
- ½ cup (1 stick) salted butter, softened
- 2 tablespoons ground cinnamon
- 1 tablespoon ground ginger
- 1 tablespoon ground cloves

Cake:

- 3 cups all-purpose flour
- 2 teaspoons baking powder
- 1 teaspoon sea salt
- 1 cup (2 sticks) salted butter, softened
- 1 cup sugar
- 1 teaspoon vanilla extract
- 3 eggs
- 1½ cups whole milk

Directions:

Filling:

In a med bowl, stir together the brown sugar, pecans, flour, butter, cinnamon, ginger, and cloves. Set aside.

Cake:

Preheat the oven to 350°F.

In a med bowl, mix the flour, baking powder, and sea salt.

In a bowl, cream together the butter and granulated sugar until pale and fluffy. Stir in the vanilla, then add the eggs, stirring well after each addition.

Add the flour mixture & the milk, alternately in thirds, to the butter mixture, stirring well after each addition, until completely combined.

Pour half the batter into the skillet. Top with half the filling. Layer the remaining batter on top. Crumble the filling over the top.

Bake for 40-45 mins, or until cooked through. Serve hot with a cup of coffee.

14. Glazed Pecan Raisin Cake

A super delicious pecan raisin cake with a sugar and orange juice glaze.

Makes: 20 servings

Prep: 2 hrs.

Cook:

Ingredients:

- 1 cup powdered sugar
- 3 cups crushed pecans
- 6 eggs
- 1 teaspoon baking powder
- 1 tablespoon orange juice + 1 teaspoon more
- 3 cups raisins
- 2 ¼ cups brown sugar
- 2 tablespoons powdered nutmeg
- 2 cups softened unsalted butter

Directions:

Preheat oven at 350 F. Oil and flour a 10-inch Bundt pan. Combine nutmeg, baking powder and flour in a bowl.

In an electric mixer bowl put brown sugar and butter and beat until fluffy. Put in egg, one at a time while beating, and beat the mixture at low speed.

Gently mix flour mixture and fold in raisins and pecans. Pour batter into the pan and bake for 1 hour 30 minutes. Invert the cake on wire rack and let it cool completely.

In a bowl mix, powdered sugar and orange juice and pour it over the cake.

Serve.

15. Baked Berry Pecan Oatmeal

Baked oatmeal is a wonderful breakfast—it's sweet, filling, and endlessly adaptable.

Makes: 4 servings

Prep: 5 mins

Cook: 45 mins

Ingredients:

- 2 cups rolled oats
- 1 cup fresh blueberries
- 1 cup fresh strawberries, halved
- ½ cup chopped pecans
- 1 tablespoon packed brown sugar
- 1 teaspoon ground cinnamon
- 1 teaspoon baking powder
- ½ teaspoon sea salt
- 2 eggs
- 1½ cups whole milk
- ¼ cup honey
- 3 tablespoons salted butter, melted

Directions:

Preheat the oven to 350°F.

In a bowl, stir together the pecans, blueberries, strawberries, oats, brown sugar, cinnamon, baking powder, and sea salt.

In a med bowl, whisk the eggs, milk, honey, and butter. Fold the milk mixture into the oat mixture. Spoon the batter into the skillet.

Bake for 40-45 mins, or until crisp around the edges and cooked through. Serve hot.

16. Caramel Popcorn with Pecans

This recipe makes enough for gift bags or movie night at home with friends and family.

Makes: 2 gallons

Prep: 20 mins

Cook: 15 mins

Ingredients:

- 3–4 tbsp. canola oil
- 1 cup popcorn kernels (20 cups popped)
- ½ cup packed brown sugar
- ½ cup (1 stick) unsalted butter
- ½ cup corn syrup
- 2 tbsp. molasses
- 2 cups unsalted, roasted pecans
- 1 (14-ounce) can sweetened condensed milk
- 1 tsp. vanilla extract
- 1 tsp. sea salt

Directions:

Preheat the oven to 350°F. Spray two 12- by 18-inch rimmed baking sheets with cooking spray and set aside.

Pour enough canola oil into a large soup pot to cover the bottom and set over medium-high heat. Add four kernels to the pot and cover. When the kernels pop, add the remaining popcorn and shake the pot to mix the kernels with the oil. Cook, shaking the pan occasionally while the corn is popping, until the pops are a few seconds apart. Move the popcorn into a very large bowl.

Combine the brown sugar, butter, corn syrup, and molasses in a large heavy-duty saucepan over medium-high heat. Bring to a boil, stirring regularly. Once it boils, cook without stirring until the mixture reaches 260°F on a candy thermometer, about 4 mins.

Remove from heat & add in the pecans. Then stir in the condensed milk, salt, and vanilla.

Return the pan to over low heat and cook for 2 minutes. Pour the warm caramel and pecan mixture over the popcorn and mix thoroughly with a large spoon. Don't use your hands, as the caramel will still be very hot.

Spread the popcorn mixture on the prepared baking sheets.

Bake for 15 minutes, stirring at the 7-minute mark. If the two trays do not fit on the same oven rack, so that you have one on an upper rack and one on a lower one, swap them when you stir the mixture.

Cool the popcorn in their pans, to room temperature, for 15 to 20 minutes. The popcorn will keep for 5 to 7 days stored in an airtight container or plastic storage bags.

17. Caramel Nut Brittle

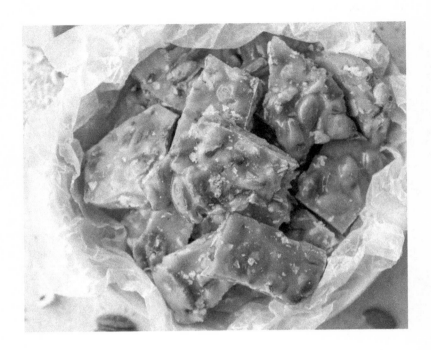

Sweet, salty, and crunchy, this caramel nut brittle has all the makings of an amazing homemade gift.

Makes: 6 servings

Prep: 10 mins

Cook: 20 mins

Ingredients:

- 2 cups white sugar
- 1 cup light corn syrup
- 1/2 cup water
- 2 tbsp. butter, plus additional for greasing
- 1 tbsp. baking soda
- 1 tbsp. vanilla extract
- 1/2 tsp salt
- 2 1/2 cup pecans

Directions:

Butter a large cookie sheet.

In a med. saucepan, combine the sugar, light corn syrup, water and butter. Using a candy thermometer, stir until it reaches 280 degrees.

Remove and then add in the nuts, baking soda, salt and vanilla extract.

Pour immediately into prepared pan and tilt so that mixture covers the entire pan.

Allow it to cool and then crack into large pieces.

18. Caramel Praline Ice Cream

Praline, a delicious crunchy caramel and nut mixture, is a very popular flavoring in France.

Makes: 6-8 servings

Prep: 2 hrs. 10 mins

Cook: 5 mins

Ingredients:

- ½ cup blanched pecans
- 7/8 cup caster sugar, divided
- 4 tbsp. water
- 1 cup heavy cream
- 6 egg yolks
- 2 cups milk

Directions:

Lightly brush a baking sheet with oil. Put the nuts in a saucepan with 1/3 cup of the sugar and the water. Boil over high heat, making sure to swirl the pan to dissolve the sugar, then boil (don't stir), for 4-5 minutes until the syrup and nuts begin to pop. Immediately pour on to the baking sheet (do not touch the hot caramel). Cool, then break into pieces.

Finely grind the praline in a food processor, using the metal blade. Or, put in a strong polythene bag and crush with a rolling pin.

Put the cream into a cold bowl and set aside. In another bowl whisk the egg yolks and remaining sugar until thick and creamy. Meanwhile, bring the milk just to a simmer over a medium heat, then whisk into the eggs and return the mixture to the saucepan.

With a wooden spoon, stir over a low heat for 3-4 minutes until the sauce thickens, then strain the custard into the bowl of cream. Cool, then chill until cold. Stir in the praline, and freeze in an ice cream maker, or in the freezer, beating once or twice until smooth.

Leave the ice cream to soften at room temperature for 5-10 minutes before serving.

19. Toffee with Chocolate and Pecans

Butter, cream and sugar come together to make caramels with dark chocolate and pecans.

Makes: about 2 pounds

Prep: 15 mins

Cook: 25 mins

Ingredients:

- 2 cups sugar
- 1 ½ cups (3 sticks) unsalted butter
- ¼ cup water
- 3 tbsp. light corn syrup
- 1 tsp. baking soda
- 1 tsp. sea salt
- 1 tsp. vanilla extract
- 12 oz. dark chocolate, coarsely chopped
- 2 cups pecans, toasted and finely chopped

Directions:

Spray a 12- by 17-inch rimmed baking sheet with cooking spray and set aside.

Combine the sugar, butter, water, and corn syrup in a large heavy-duty saucepan and bring to a boil over medium-high heat. When the mixture begins to boil, brush down the insides of the pan with a damp pastry brush. Then reduce the heat to med. to keep the sugar mixture at a steady boil until it reaches 285°F. This may take 10 minutes or more. Do not stir.

When the sugar mixture reaches 285°F, remove the pan from the heat and stir in the baking soda, salt, and vanilla extract. Keep stirring until the bubbling stops.

Pour onto baking sheet and spread it evenly with the back of a wooden spoon or an offset-handle metal spatula.

Scatter the chocolate pieces evenly over the surface of the hot toffee. Let this sit for a few minutes, until the chocolate has melted. Spread the melted chocolate evenly across the entire surface of the toffee.

Gently scatter a thin layer of pecans over the melted chocolate. You want a thin layer because only the pecans that are actually touching the chocolate will stick to it. The rest will just fall off.

Let cool for 10 to 15 minutes. You can then break it up by hand and store it in an airtight container or a plastic storage bag at room temperature; it will keep for 7 to 10 days.

20. Chocolate Banana Pecan Bread

Instead of tossing away those ripened bananas, use them to make this ultra-moist, double chocolate banana pecan bread. Perfect for both breakfast and dessert!

Makes: 1 loaf

Prep: 10 mins

Cook: 50 mins

Ingredients:

- 1 cup all-purpose flour
- 1/2 cup unsweetened cocoa powder
- 1/2 tsp. salt
- 1 tsp. baking soda
- 3 medium-large ripe bananas
- ½ stick unsalted butter, melted
- 4 tbsp. vegetable oil
- 3/4 cup brown sugar
- 2 tbsp. milk
- 1 egg
- 1 tsp. vanilla extract
- 1 cup dark chocolate chips, divided
- ½ cup roasted pecans, chopped

Directions:

Preheat the oven to 350°F. Lightly grease a loaf pan.

In a med-sized bowl, combine the dry ingredients and set aside.

In a large bowl, mix together the mashed bananas, butter, oil, eggs and vanilla extract. Add in the flour mixture and whisk until just combined. Fold in ¾ cup of chocolate chips along with the pecans.

Pour batter & top with remaining chocolate chips. Bake for about 45-50 mins.

Serve.

21. White Chocolate Pecan Blondies

Take a break from regular brownies and enjoy these gooey, moist and absolutely delicious white chocolate blondies.

Makes: 12 servings

Prep: 5 mins

Cook: 30 mins

Ingredients:

- 2 sticks unsalted butter
- 4 large eggs
- 1 1/2 cups white sugar
- ½ cup brown sugar
- 1 tsp. vanilla extract
- 2 cups all-purpose flour
- 1 tsp. salt
- 1 1/4 cups white chocolate chips
- 1 cup roasted pecans
- Vanilla ice cream, for serving

Directions:

Preheat the oven to 325°F. Line a 9x13 inch baking pan with baking paper and set aside.

In a medium-sized bowl, melt together the butter and white chocolate chips in a microwave in 20 second intervals. Set aside to cool.

In a bowl, beat the eggs, white sugar, brown sugar and vanilla extract until well combined. Add in the butter mixture followed by the flour and salt and beat again until just combined. Add in the pecans.

Pour mixture and bake for about 30 mins.

Serve with vanilla ice cream.

22. Caramelized Brussels Sprout Hash with Crumbled Bacon and Pecans

This is such a great way to cook brussels sprouts. The apple juice gives this dish its sweetness, the lemon juice adds more flavor and helps the brussels sprouts retain their green color, and the pecans help give the dish more texture.

Makes: 8 servings

Prep:

Cook:

Ingredients:

- 3 strips thick-sliced bacon (optional)
- 3 tablespoon butter
- 2 cups sliced brussels sprouts, rinsed, ends slightly trimmed, and cut into ¼-inch slices
- ¼ cup apple juice or cider
- ¼ cup water
- 1 teaspoon lemon juice
- ¼ teaspoon lemon zest
- Salt and freshly ground black pepper

Directions:

In a 10- or 12-inch cast iron skillet over medium heat, add the bacon strips and cook until crisp. Move to a plate.

Wipe skillet, and then add the butter. Once it has melted, add the brussels sprouts and cook for 2 minutes. Add the apple juice & water, cover, and cook for 3 minutes. Uncover, increase the heat to med-high, and cook, gently stirring occasionally, for 3 minutes more, or until any moisture has been absorbed. Add the lemon juice. Reduce & cook for 5 minutes without stirring. Sprinkle the lemon zest over the brussels sprouts, season them with salt and pepper, and cook, carefully flipping the sprouts with a spatula from time to time, for 2 to 3 minutes, or until golden brown.

Remove, crumble the bacon over the brussels sprouts, and serve.

23. Dried Fruit Pecan Oatmeal

Delicious and filling oatmeal recipe with pecans and dried fruit.

Makes: 6 servings

Prep:

Cook:

Ingredients:

- 6 cups water
- ½ tsp salt
- 3 ¼ cups quick cooking oats
- 3/4 cup brown sugar
- ½ cup maple syrup
- ½ cup chopped almonds
- ½ cup dried fruit

Directions:

In a shallow 12" Dutch oven, bring water and salt to a rolling boil over 10 hot coals. While waiting for water, mix remaining ingredients together in a small mixing bowl. When water boils, stir in oats.

Continue cooking and stirring for one minute. Remove from fire and top with fruit and nut mixture.

Serve hot with milk or cream.

24. Salted Caramel Pecan Milkshake

A delightful combination of sweet and salty caramel and pecan milkshake that tastes like melted toffee in your mouth.

Makes: 6 servings

Prep: 25 mins

Ingredients:

For the Caramel Sauce:

- 2 tbsp water
- ½ cup white sugar
- 1/3 cup heavy cream
- 1 ½ tbsp. unsalted butter, cut into squares
- ½ tsp vanilla extract
- ½ tsp sea salt

For the Milkshake:

- 2 1/2 cups vanilla ice cream
- 2 cups butter pecan ice cream
- 3 cups whole milk
- 1 ½ tsp vanilla extract
- Whipped cream, for topping
- Sea salt, for topping
- Chopped pecans, for topping

Directions:

Place sugar & water in a medium-sized saucepan over medium-high heat. Stir the mixture constantly until it just starts to boil. Stop stirring and increase heat. When the mixture turns into an amber color (5-10 minutes), remove & slowly add in the cream, whisking constantly. Add in the butter and whisk again. Add in the vanilla & salt and whisk until combined.

Allow to cool to room temperature.

Place vanilla ice cream, butter pecan ice cream, milk, vanilla extract and caramel sauce in a blender and blend until smooth.

Divide between glasses & top with whipped cream, a pinch of sea salt and pecans.

25. Coconut Pecan Granola

Sprinkle this delicious granola on your oatmeal or on top of your smoothie bowls.

Makes: 5 cups

Prep: 10 mins

Cook: 25 mins

Ingredients:

- 2 cups rolled oats
- ½ cup flaked coconut
- ½ cup pecans, chopped
- 3 tbsp. honey

Directions:

Preheat the oven to 300°F.

Combine together the oats, coconut, pecan, and honey in a large baking pan.

Bake or 15 minutes. Remove and stir and then bake for 10 minutes more. Cool.

Store granola in an air-tight container.

26. Peanut Butter Pecan Fudge

A delicious 3-ingredient fudge recipe with crunchy pecans and luscious peanut butter.

Makes: 12 servings

Prep: 5 mins plus chilling time

Cook: 1 min

Ingredients:

- 1 14-ounce tub vanilla frosting
- 1 ½ cups creamy peanut butter
- ½ cup pecans, cut into halves

Directions:

Prep an 8X8 inch pan with foil and grease lightly with cooking spray.

In a large bowl, combine the peanut butter and vanilla frosting. Microwave for 1 min and mix until smooth. Add in the pecan halves and stir again until incorporated.

Pour mixture into the baking dish.

Cover and refrigerate for 2 hrs. Slice and serve.

27. Triple Chocolate Pecan Cookies

Get thrice the amount of chocolate in one bite with these soft, chewy, crunchy and insanely addicting triple chocolate chip pecan cookie recipe!

Makes: 9 servings

Prep: 30 mins

Cook: 10 mins

Ingredients:

- 4 tbsp. unsalted butter, room temperature
- 6 tbsp. white sugar
- 2 tbsp. brown sugar
- 1 small egg
- ½ + 1/8 tsp. vanilla extract
- ½ cup all-purpose flour
- ¼ tsp. salt
- ¼ + 1/8 tsp. baking powder
- 3 tbsp. unsweetened cocoa powder
- ¼ + 1/8 tsp. baking soda
- ¼ cup milk chocolate chips
- ¼ cup dark chocolate chips
- ½ cup toasted pecans

Directions:

In a bowl, beat together the 4 tbsp of softened butter and sugars for 3 minutes. Add in the egg, vanilla extract and milk beat until well combined.

In a bowl, combine all the of dry ingredients.

Working in batches of three, add the dry mixture to the butter mixture and beat until just combined. Fold in the chocolate chips and pecans. Cover and refrigerate for 20 minutes.

Preheat the oven to 350°F. Line and grease a baking pan with baking paper.

Scoop out 2 tablespoons of dough for each cookie and place on pan. Bake for 8-14 minutes or until the edges of the cookies are crisp.

Serve.

28. Vanilla Pecan Milkshake

Creamy, rich and delicious, this vanilla and pecan milkshake is out-of-this-world good!

Makes: 6 servings

Prep: 10 mins

Ingredients:

- 2 1/2 cups vanilla ice cream
- 2 cups butter pecan ice cream
- 3 cups whole milk
- 1 ½ tsp vanilla extract
- Whipped cream, for topping
- Toasted pecans, for topping

Directions:

Place the vanilla ice cream, butter pecan ice cream, milk and vanilla extract in a blender and blend until thoroughly combined and smooth.

Divide between glasses & top with whipped cream and pecans.

Serve.

29. Spiced Banana Pecan Bread

Banana bread recipe with cinnamon, cardamom and pecans.

Makes: 1 loaf

Prep: 10 mins

Cook: 50 mins

Ingredients:

- 1 cup all-purpose flour
- 1/4 cup unsweetened cocoa powder
- 1/2 tsp. salt
- 1 tsp. baking soda
- ½ tsp cinnamon
- ¼ tsp cardamom powder
- 3 medium-large ripe bananas
- ½ stick unsalted butter, melted
- 4 tbsp. vegetable oil
- 3/4 cup brown sugar
- 2 tbsp. milk
- 1 egg
- 1 tsp. vanilla extract
- ½ cup roasted pecans, chopped

Directions:

Preheat the oven to 350°F. Lightly grease a loaf pan.

In a med-sized bowl, combine the dry ingredients and set aside.

In a large bowl, mix together the mashed bananas, butter, oil, eggs and vanilla extract. Add in the flour mixture and whisk until just combined. Fold in the pecans.

Pour batter in the pan. Bake for about 45-50 mins.

Serve.

30. Coffee Pecan Milkshake

The perfect drink to help you going in the summer (or any other season really), this coffee pecan milkshake is rich, favorful and oh-so-creamy.

Makes: 6 servings

Prep: 10 mins

Ingredients:

For the Ganache (optional but recommended):

- ½ cup heavy cream
- 6 tbsp. semi-sweet chocolate chips

For the Milkshake:

- 5 cups cold-brewed coffee
- 2 1/2 cups vanilla ice cream
- 2 cups butter pecan ice cream
- 3 cups whole milk
- Whipped cream, for topping

Directions:

For the Ganache:

Place the heavy cream in a medium-sized bowl and microwave for about 30 seconds or until cream just starts to boil. Quickly add in the chocolate chips and whisk until smooth and no lumps remain. Heat for a few seconds more if needed. Set aside to cool slightly.

For the Milkshake:

Place coffee, ice cream, milk and ganache in a blender and blend until smooth and creamy.

Divide between glasses & top with whipped cream.

Conclusion

Well there you have it! 30 delicious and easy pecan recipes for you to try. Make sure to stock up on pecans and then try out all 30 recipes – and remember to leave some for your friends and family!

About the Author

Allie Allen developed her passion for the culinary arts at the tender age of five when she would help her mother cook for their large family of 8. Even back then, her family knew this would be more than a hobby for the young Allie and when she graduated from high school, she applied to cooking school in London. It had always been a dream of the young chef to study with some of Europe's best and she made it happen by attending the Chef Academy of London.

After graduation, Allie decided to bring her skills back to North America and open up her own restaurant. After 10 successful years as head chef and owner, she decided to sell her business and pursue other career avenues. This monumental decision led Allie to her true calling, teaching. She also started to write e-books for her students to study at home for practice. She is now the proud author of several e-books and gives private and semi-private cooking lessons to a range of students at all levels of experience.

Stay tuned for more from this dynamic chef and teacher when she releases more informative e-books on cooking and baking in the near future. Her work is infused with stores and anecdotes you will love!

Author's Afterthoughts

I can't tell you how grateful I am that you decided to read my book. My most heartfelt thanks that you took time out of your life to choose my work and I hope you find benefit within these pages.

There are so many books available today that offer similar content so that makes it even more humbling that you decided to buying mine.

Tell me what you thought! I am eager to hear your opinion and ideas on what you read as are others who are looking for a good book to buy. Leave a review on Amazon.com so others can benefit from your wisdom!

With much thanks,

Allie Allen

CPSIA information can be obtained
at www.ICGtesting.com
Printed in the USA
LVHW111049071019
633401LV00006B/1462/P

9 781694 720665